Philippians

Paul's Letter to His Partners

Andrew Wommack

Published in partnership between Andrew Wommack Ministries and Harrison House Publishers.

Woodland Park, CO 80863 – Shippensburg, PA 17257

ISBN 13 TP: 978-1-59548-663-9

For Worldwide Distribution, Printed in the USA

1 2 3 4 5 6 / 27 26 25 24

Contents

Introduction

Paul is one of the greatest examples in scripture of someone who suffered greatly yet always rejoiced in the Lord (Phil. 4:4). Paul wrote the book of Philippians from prison, after being incarcerated for at least three years at that time. Yet this is the most joyful of all Paul's letters. He still had joy in the midst of a very trying situation.

How did he do that?

The book of Philippians gives us insight into the heart of this man who had learned to be content in whatever situation he found himself in (Phil. 4:11). Paul bares his soul to his partners and gives us keys to his life of success. The same principles that worked for him will work for us too, if we will work them. Paul went on to change the world. His writings were the key to the Reformation, and they are still setting people free 2,000 years later.

Praise the Lord that He inspired Paul to share his heart with his partners and reveal what made him the man he was. We would do well to examine what he says and follow his example.

1 Corinthians 10:11 says,

Now all these things happened unto them for ensamples: and they are written for our admonition, upon whom the ends of the world are come.

The Word of God shows not only the good things people accomplished, but also all the bad things they went through. It's not whitewashed. God did this for our benefit so that we could learn from the people we read about in the Bible. We don't have to learn everything by hard knocks.

Paul went through all kinds of hardships and persecutions for the Gospel's sake, and yet he stayed encouraged, thankful, and kept praising God. Paul is probably one of the greatest men who ever walked the face of the earth, considering the things God did in his life.

In his epistle (or letter) to the church at Philippi, Paul reached out and encouraged those who had regularly given to him—his partners! At a time when he could have been complaining about being imprisoned at Rome, he instead thought enough of his partners to write to them, thank them for their generosity, remind them of what he had taught them, and encourage them to receive the rewards of their faithfulness.

You and I wouldn't be where we are today if it wasn't for Paul's revelation of grace. And the book of Philippians is one of the most joyful letters Paul ever wrote. He loved the Philippians and was thankful for their partnership. And because of that, this little letter includes some of the most amazing things you'll ever read!

Chapter 1

Paul Had a Revelation

Paul and Timotheus, the servants of Jesus Christ, to all the saints in Christ Jesus which are at Philippi, with the bishops and deacons.

Philippians 1:1

Paul was a student of the well-known Jewish rabbi Gamaliel (Acts 22:3) and called himself a *"Hebrew of the Hebrews"* and *"as touching the law, a Pharisee"* (Phil. 3:5). This guy was steeped in religion. As a result, Paul (then, Saul of Tarsus) was so brutal that he held the clothes of the men who stoned Stephen to death (Acts 7:58–59). After that, he began to persecute the church (Acts 8:1–3). But when he encountered the Lord on the road to Damascus, it transformed his life (Acts 9:3–6).

Paul spent three years in the desert after his salvation (Gal. 1:17–18), trying to figure out how Jesus fit in with everything he had learned in the Old Testament. In the end, he came out preaching the Gospel and teaching concepts so radical that even Peter said they were hard to understand.

You see, Peter didn't really have a revelation of the Gospel like Paul. That's a strong statement, but Peter didn't fully understand God's grace the way Paul did. As a matter of fact, Paul wound up rebuking Peter to his face when he lost sight of what God had already shown him about grace (Gal. 2:11).

Peter had spent three and a half years with Jesus in His physical body, saw His miracles, and heard all His teaching. But even he said,

Our beloved brother Paul also according to the wisdom given unto him hath written unto you; As also in all his *epistles, speaking in them of these things; in which are some things hard to be understood, which they that are unlearned and unstable wrest, as* they do *also the other* **scriptures**.

2 Peter 3:15–16

Peter called Paul's writings *"scriptures"* in his day. Paul ended up writing half of the books of the New Testament. That's awesome!

On top of that, Paul suffered persecution, but he viewed it as just a *"light affliction"* (2 Cor. 4:17). In 2 Corinthians 11:23–30, Paul lists some of his light afflictions. He was beaten with rods and whips multiple times, stoned, left for dead, imprisoned, and shipwrecked. When Paul went to a town, instead of checking in to a hotel, he probably just stopped by the prison and said, "Save a spot for me, because I'll be back!" As a matter of fact, he wrote to the Philippians while in prison.

He suffered hunger, cold, nakedness and everything mentioned above for the sake of the Gospel. Considering all that, when I study Philippians, I think about what an honor it is to have Paul's writings. Through them, we get a glimpse into a person's life who has literally transformed the world.

'Fellowship in the Gospel'

Grace be *unto you, and peace, from God our Father, and* from *the Lord Jesus Christ.*

Philippians 1:2

You don't get peace until you understand grace. That's why Paul could be joyful and praise God, even while he was in prison (Acts 16:25–26). If you are still in performance mode, trying to please God through your works, and thinking that He moves in your life according to your own goodness, you'll never have peace with God.

Romans 5:1 says we have peace with God because we are justified by faith. So, peace comes because of what Jesus has already done, not because of what we're doing. Some people are so wrapped up in themselves and so focused on what they are doing that they stop the flow of God's power and peace in their lives.

> *I thank my God upon every remembrance of you, always in every prayer of mine for you all making request with joy, for your fellowship in the gospel from the first day until now.*

Philippians 1:3–5

Now, I don't believe Paul thanked God for every single person he ministered to. Some of those people gave him great grief. Over the years I've spent in ministry, I've met a lot of great people, and many have even become good friends. But there are some people I don't thank God for every time I think about them!

Paul was thanking God for the church at Philippi because of their partnership. The word *"fellowship"* in these verses is translated from the Greek word *koinonia*,[1] which also means *partnership*. He is thanking God for them supporting him in the Gospel.

We don't know exactly how long Paul ministered, but it may have been thirty years or more. And Paul said in Phil. 4:15-16 that the Philippians were the only ones who supported him after he left their area. That's amazing! Paul suffered hardship as very few ministers have in order to spread the good news of Jesus' salvation, and yet only one church supported him in his journeys. He even had to make tents in many places, working a secular job to support himself and the people who traveled with him (Acts 18:3).

I'm sure that's one of the main reasons Paul thanked God every time he thought of the Philippians. They were his partners. They had helped him on numerous occasions and once again, their support for him came to him in Rome. How else could a prisoner pay for a hired house for two years (Acts 28:30)?

The Philippians partnership with Paul is a major influence on Paul's statements and promises in this letter.

'Partakers of My Grace'

Being confident of this very thing, that he which hath begun a good work in you will perform it until the day of Jesus Christ: Even as it is meet for me to think this of you all, because I have you in my heart; inasmuch as both in my bonds, and in the defence and confirmation of the gospel, ye all are partakers of my grace.

Philippians 1:6–7

I hear people use this all the time and say, "I am confident that God is going to continue the good work that He began in me." I agree that God wants to do this for everybody, but He isn't able to because it takes participation on our part. These Philippians were exceptional people who weren't only thinking of themselves. They proved that by sending to Paul's necessities in Thessalonica twice (Phil. 4:15) and again during his imprisonment in Rome. They had gone beyond what they could get for themselves and were into giving so that others could receive. That's partnership.

Many Christians get stuck at the front door of salvation and don't enter into the fulness of what Jesus provided. They stay focused on themselves and their needs and don't get into the true heart of Christianity about laying down our lives for others and the Gospel. Partnership will shake us out of that self-centeredness and usher us into a deeper realm of relationship with the Lord that isn't about what we can get, but what we can give. Jesus said that our hearts would follow our treasure (Matt. 6:21).

It was also right for Paul to express that confidence toward the Philippians because they were in his heart. He prayed for them and loved them. He was their partner too. They had received the same grace he had received. He knew God was completing the work begun in him, so that same grace and Holy Spirit would accomplish the same in them. That's just amazing!

Paul was saying that these Philippians were partaking of the grace that was upon his life. You could even say that all of us today are receiving from God because of the grace that was upon Paul's life and the time that he spent getting and recording revelation from God. This has been the foundation of Christianity for the last 2,000 years.

When Martin Luther got a revelation, put his ninety-five theses on the door, and started the Reformation, it was based on what Paul had done. As he was climbing up the steps on his knees at the Vatican, it dawned on him that *the just shall live by faith*" (Rom. 1:17). The grace that was on Paul 1,500 years earlier changed Luther's life and caused the Reformation.

We need to recognize what would've happened if Paul had just kept everything to himself and hadn't written down his revelation. If he had said when he was persecuted, "It's not worth it," and just quit, we would be lost today! I am totally dependent upon God, and if I didn't have the revelation of the Word, I wouldn't know how to do anything. What a blessing!

We are all partakers of the grace that was upon Paul's life. In a similar way, the grace that is on your life, the salvation that you've received, and the revelation God has given you is not for you to keep to yourself. We've often heard it said that you are the only Bible that some people are ever going to read. You pass by people every single day that need what you have. People need the grace that is on your life, and you need to boldly share your faith with others.

Go Deeper Than the Surface

For God is my record, how greatly I long after you all in the bowels of Jesus Christ. And this I pray, that your love may abound yet more and more in knowledge and in all judgment.

Philippians 1:8–9

Most people know God loves them, but do not understand that His love is not one-dimensional. In Ephesians 3:18–19, Paul prayed,

> [That you] *may be able to comprehend with all saints what* is *the breadth, and length, and depth, and height; and to know the love of Christ, which passeth knowledge, that ye might be filled with all the fulness of God.*

The love of God is multi-dimensional, but most people only think about it on a surface level.

One of the largest gold strikes in the world was in Colorado, near our Charis Bible College campus. Millions of dollars' worth of gold was discovered, but it was mostly *placer* gold. That's gold that was washed out in the streams and could be found on the surface of the ground. It didn't take very long to find all the placer gold. So, people started digging mines.

There is now a mine in Cripple Creek, Colorado, where they dug up *a mountain*, hauled it off, and put chemicals on rock piles to draw out silver and gold and other minerals. This was a huge mountain that used to have a road that went around it, and now it's just rubble. But they are finding three to four times as much gold *in* the ground as there ever was *on top* of the ground!

It's the same thing with the love of God. Most Christians just pick out the easy things, but they don't plumb the depths. There are people who will say, "Oh, I know God loves me," and then in the next breath they'll turn around and say, "God put this sickness on me to teach me something," or, "God killed my child to humble me." No! That's not God's love!

Love doesn't increase through prayer, having somebody lay hands on you, going to church, or paying your tithes. God's kind of love only increases proportional to our knowledge of what He has done for us. The knowledge that is being spoken of in these verses is spiritual understanding of God's love. Judgment is the ability to use or apply that knowledge correctly.

'Be Sincere and Without Offense'

That ye may approve things that are excellent; that ye may be sincere and without offence till the day of Christ.

Philippians 1:10

Paul was saying that as we gain spiritual understanding of God's love and learn to apply it correctly in our relationships, then the manifestation of God's love in our lives will increase dramatically. This leads to better discernment about right and wrong and produces sincerity that results in us walking without offense.

Another result of getting a greater understanding of the love of God is that you will approve things that are excellent. We have so many people today who can't even figure out which restroom to go into. How do people become this confused? Well, it's because they don't know the love of God. They just don't understand God or approve of what is excellent and godly.

The word *sincere* used here comes from the Greek word, *eilikrines*, which means "judged by sunlight, i.e. tested as genuine (figuratively):—pure, sincere."[2] It means sun tested. People would have clay pots and if a crack formed in them it would ruin the pots. Instead of replacing the pot as they should, they would put wax over the crack, repaint the whole pot, and sell it as if it was still good. But when the sun came out, the wax would melt and expose the pot's flaws.

This is saying that you would be sincere—sun tested—so that even under heat and pressure you wouldn't break. Paul is saying you wouldn't have all these flaws, but *"be sincere and without offence."* People who only cover up their flaws to portray something to others that they aren't, are called hypocrites. None of us want to be hypocrites.

Being filled with the fruits of righteousness, which are by Jesus Christ, unto the glory and praise of God.

Philippians 1:11

All the fruits of righteousness come from God's love. If we want more fruit, we need to focus more on the love of God. This goes back to our love abounding more and more through knowledge and judgment. When that happens, our recognition of what is excellent changes, hypocrisy leaves, and sin leaves too. This verse reveals that this will also produce righteous fruit that glorifies and praises God. Any "love" that doesn't cause all these things isn't God's true love.

Priority on the Gospel

But I would ye should understand, brethren, that the things which happened unto me have fallen out rather unto the furtherance of the gospel.

Philippians 1:12

Paul had been persecuted (2 Cor. 11:23–27), and he suffered more than just about anybody. Yet here he is saying all these things have worked together for the Gospel.

He was imprisoned in Rome and had spent at least three years in prison at this time. But he's writing to people who loved him and he's trying to console them. Now, if you had been put in prison unjustly, gone through a shipwreck (Acts 27:27–28:5), and had suffered the way Paul did, would you be thinking about somebody else and wanting to make sure they wouldn't worry about you?

Many people would be so focused on themselves—griping and complaining about the things that happened to them—that they wouldn't even think about anybody else. But Paul wrote this entire book because he was concerned about his partners first. He loved these people, and he knew they would be worried about him.

You see, the Philippians didn't have access to communication the way we do. They couldn't call Paul. They couldn't send him a text message. It took months for word to get back to Philippi from Rome. So, Paul was concerned because these people were wondering about how he was doing. Instead of thinking just about himself, Paul was ministering to these people. He was the one suffering, yet he was thinking about other people.

Paul said in 1 Corinthians 11:1,

Be ye followers of me, even as I also am *of Christ.*

This is an attitude that we ought to be emulating. We ought to be thinking about other people instead of ourselves.

Those who only think about themselves often are obsessed with what they want but don't have. Getting out of ourselves and seeing others' problems often helps us recognize how blessed we really are.

Years ago, when I was in Mexico, I visited a trash dump. I met people there who were between forty and fifty years old, and they had lived at that dump their entire lives. They were born in a cardboard box, lived in a shack, and ate from the trash that came to the dump. When you see somebody living like that, you'll find your own situation isn't as bad as you thought! It's like the person who complained about the pain in his feet until he met somebody who didn't have any feet.

When I was in the Baptist church, they had a song that went, "Count your many blessings, name them one by one, and it will surprise you what the Lord has done."[3] If you take your eyes off of yourself and start thinking about other people, it'll change your whole attitude! You'll think about your blessings more than your problems.

'Speak the Word Without Fear'

So that my bonds in Christ are manifest in all the palace, and in all other places; *And many of the brethren in the Lord, waxing confident by my bonds, are much more bold to speak the word without fear.*

Philippians 1:13–14

Courage is contagious. When you get around somebody who's standing strong, it inspires you. It can build you up. In Paul's day, many of the brethren became confident in their faith by seeing the way he stood for the defense of the Gospel, such as when he was on trial before Nero, the Roman emperor (Acts 25–26, 2 Tim. 4:16–17).

In Caesar's household, people heard about this crazy guy who was standing before Nero, saying Jesus Christ died for the sins of the whole world and that on the third day He rose again. Those people told others what they heard Paul preach, but not everyone had the same motive.

Some indeed preach Christ even of envy and strife; and some also of good will: The one preach Christ of contention, not sincerely, supposing to add affliction to my

> *bonds: But the other of love, knowing that I am set for*
> *the defence of the gospel.*

Philippians 1:15–17

Some people were probably mocking Paul and thinking that what he was doing would only make his situation worse. But Paul was so in love with God he didn't care whether they mocked him or not. He was just rejoicing that people were hearing about Jesus and what He had done.

Years ago, our friend Jesse Duplantis had a lot of criticism come against his ministry because the media misquoted him about believing for an airplane. But Jesse told me, "There is no such thing as bad publicity!" Regardless of people's motives, the news of what Jesse was believing for got out, and that worked to his benefit.

Jesse didn't even try to correct what was being said about his ministry, because it was actually furthering the message of the Gospel. His income went up 20 percent because so many people were talking about him. And wouldn't you know it, his ministry ended up getting that airplane debt free! Praise the Lord!

You can get to a place where you and your reputation are not the most important things in your life. And it really frees you up! I'll tell you, if criticism could kill a person, I'd be dead. But, to me, it's just like water off a duck's back. You can only get to that point by putting God first.

What then? notwithstanding, every way, whether in pretence, or in truth, Christ is preached; and I therein do rejoice, yea, and will rejoice. For I know that this shall turn to my salvation through your prayer, and the supply of the Spirit of Jesus Christ.

Philippians 1:18–19

Remember, Paul wrote to the Philippians while he was imprisoned. There are eighteen times in the four chapters of this epistle (*King James Version*) where Paul used the words joy,[4] rejoice,[5] rejoicing,[6] or rejoiced.[7] This was probably the happiest book that Paul ever wrote because he was rejoicing even while he was in prison.

The only reason Paul was able to rejoice like that was because he put Jesus and others ahead of himself. We can do the same thing.

'With All Boldness'

According to my earnest expectation and my *hope, that*

21

in nothing I shall be ashamed, but that with all bold-ness, as always, so now also Christ shall be magnified in my body, whether it be by life, or by death.

Philippians 1:20

Paul had been faithful for such a long time, but here he was, saying that he wanted to have boldness as he always did. Boldness had been part of his life since his conversion, but it didn't come automatically. Here he was, towards the end of his life still seeking to be bold in his defense of the Gospel.

Boldness was important for many others in the Bible, such as King David. When David killed Goliath (1 Sam. 17), nobody believed he could do it. Even King Saul made fun of him, but David said, *"The Lord that delivered me out of the paw of the lion, and out of the paw of the bear, he will deliver me out of the hand of this Philistine"* (1 Sam. 17:37).

God gave him the strength to kill a lion and a bear on the backside of the desert when nobody was watching. He could've run away—and nobody would've blamed him—but he put his life on the line and stood strong when the grandstands were empty. Because of those things, David had the boldness to say, *"this uncircumcised Philistine shall be as one of them"* (1 Sam. 17:36).

Everybody wants to kill Goliath, but nobody wants to kill the lion and the bear first. You have to develop boldness and learn to be faithful in little things before you are trusted with more. It's not because God doesn't love you. It's because He loves you so much that he doesn't want to put you in a position where you're going to be attacked by Satan when you don't have what it takes to stand.

Not long after the Lord touched my life on March 23, 1968, God showed me how we would have a worldwide ministry. But in the early years, people stayed away from our meetings by the thousands! I just couldn't see how we could get from where we were to where God wanted us to be.

Today, we have the potential to reach more than 5 billion people around the world through our *Gospel Truth* television program. We've also graduated thousands of people through our Charis Bible College who are taking the Gospel to people I'll never reach. But if God had put the full responsibility of these things on me fifty years ago—or even twenty years ago—it may have destroyed me!

You see, I had to put down roots. The Lord showed me early on that, if I was a tree, the first storm that came along would knock me down. I had to sow the Word of God into my heart so I would grow on the inside—deep below the surface.

Now, our ministry is growing at an exponential rate, but that would not have been possible if had not been responsible in the little things first.

If you are not mature enough to handle more responsibilities, God won't promote you and give you greater influence because he doesn't want to destroy you. He also doesn't want the people you're influencing to be destroyed if you fail. So, it may be that God is holding you back because he loves you so much. You just aren't ready yet. Be faithful and bold in whatever God has assigned to you today, no matter how small.

'To Live Is Christ'

For to me to live is *Christ, and to die* is *gain.*

Philippians 1:21

Here was Paul, a man who had been through so much, and this was the secret to his life: *"to live* is *Christ, and to die* is *gain."* Later in this epistle, Paul talks about how all his great accomplishments were like dung compared to knowing Christ (Phil. 3:8). This attitude made Paul the person he was. He loved God more than he loved himself.

24

During the pandemic response of 2020, the government declared that churches were nonessential and tried to stop people from worshiping. We even received a cease-and-desist letter during one of our events at Charis Bible College.

My ministry staff had a war room going nearly twenty-four hours a day, making plans in case the authorities came to arrest me. I had people ask me, "What if they shut you down? What if they threaten to take away your 501c3 nonprofit status?" But worrying about what could happen is not how I live.

It's not my responsibility to consider what somebody else does. All I've got control over is myself. And I'm only going to do what God tells me to do. So, if they had put me in jail, that's their problem. I'd just start a jail ministry and get everybody in the jail saved! I'm not going to evaluate what God wants me to do based on what the consequences may be.

As it turned out, the State of Colorado sued us, and we sued them back. Eventually, the U.S. Supreme Court ruled in favor of churches in other states who fought back against lockdowns. And because of that, the State of Colorado backed down. During that time our income increased dramatically, more people became familiar with our ministry, and our impact with the Gospel grew. That's awesome!

Many Christians may know what God wants them to do but they don't always obey. Instead, their actions are based on what they think the consequences would be. If they think something bad might happen by following God's plan, they won't do it. That's not the attitude that Paul had.

During the pandemic, I had a guy come to me who was a nurse. He said the hospital he worked at told him he would be fired if he didn't take the vaccine. And I asked, "Well, do you think you're supposed to take the vaccine?" He said, "No! God told me not to do it." (Now, I'm not even discussing whether you should or shouldn't take a vaccine. I'm just saying God told *him* not to take the vaccine.)

I said, "Well, if God told you not to do it, don't do it." His immediate response was, "But they're going to fire me!" And I said, "What does that matter? If God tells you to do something, you just do it!" It's so much easier to obey God when we're like Paul and love Christ more than ourselves. There's only one God and you are not Him. If we know the Lord wants us to do something and we refuse to do it, that's making ourself God. That's idolatry.

John Quincy Adams, the sixth president of the United States, is popularly believed to have said, "Duty is ours; results are God's."[8] We should never debate doing what the Lord has instructed us to do because of a fear of what might happen. We can only live that way if we come to the same conclusion that Paul did, *"for me to live is Christ, to die is gain."*

'More Needful for You'

But if I live in the flesh, this is *the fruit of my labour: yet what I shall choose I wot not. For I am in a strait betwixt two, having a desire to depart, and to be with Christ; which is far better: Nevertheless to abide in the flesh* is *more needful for you.*

Philippians 1:22–24

Remember that Paul was writing this from prison. *"This* is *the fruit of my labour"* is referring to his imprisonment. He said in Acts 20:23 that everywhere he went, the Holy Spirit witnessed that bonds and afflictions awaited him. Paul had suffered immensely, and he longed to be with God so much that dying and going to be with the Lord seemed to be the best thing. But, again, he was not just serving himself. Paul realized it was *"more needful"* for the Philippians that he stay and continue ministering to them.

And having this confidence, I know that I shall abide and continue with you all for your furtherance and joy of faith; that your rejoicing may be more abundant in Jesus Christ for me by my coming to you again.

Philippians 1:25–26

What a great attitude! But very few people today even entertain this kind of thought. Most people believe that they are the center of the universe. They think all they have to do is stand in one place while holding a lightbulb and it'll automatically screw itself in because the world revolves around them. That's an immature attitude!

When you were born into this world, you didn't care that your mother had been up all night long giving birth. You'd just cry and wake up everybody in the house when you wanted something. A baby doesn't care about anybody but themselves. They will throw a fit, make noise, and do all kinds of things to get what they want. When you're just a week old that's understandable, but not when you're forty, fifty, or sixty years old!

When a lawyer asked Jesus about the *"great commandment in the law"* (Matt. 22:36) He answered,

Thou shalt love the Lord thy God with all thy heart, and with all thy soul, and with all thy mind. This is the first

28

and great commandment. And the second is like unto it,
Thou shalt love thy neighbour as thyself.

Matthew 22:37–39

Jesus was quoting from Leviticus 19:18. But then, Jesus said in John 13:34,

A new commandment I give unto you, That ye love
one another; as I have loved you, that ye also love one
another.

There's something better than loving your neighbor as yourself. Jesus loved us more than He loved Himself and told us to love one another *as He loved us*. That's what Paul is talking about in this letter.

This isn't oppressive. This is freedom. It's actually in losing your life that you really discover what life is all about (Matt. 10:39; 16:25). When you put other people first, you'll find out it's more blessed to give than it is to receive (Acts 20:35).

'Stand Fast in One Spirit'

Only let your conversation be as it becometh the gospel
of Christ: that whether I come and see you, or else be

29

absent, I may hear of your affairs, that ye stand fast in one spirit, with one mind striving together for the faith of the gospel.

Philippians 1:27

Paul wanted us to be of the same mind and of the same judgment. The disunity in the body of Christ today is terrible. We've got so many Christians in the United States, that if they would unite and stand together, we could solve every problem in this nation. But so many Christians will pray on Sunday, *"Thy kingdom come. Thy will be done in earth as* it is *in heaven"* (Matt. 6:10), and then turn around on a Tuesday and vote contrary to everything the Word of God says. That's not right!

We need unity in the body of Christ (Ps. 133:3). We can't control others, but we should make every effort to walk in love and unity with our brothers and sisters to the degree that we can (Rom. 12:18).

And in nothing terrified by your adversaries: which is to them an evident token of perdition, but to you of salvation, and that of God.

Philippians 1:28

30

It's a little wordy in the *King James Version*, but what Paul is saying is that you shouldn't be afraid to speak the truth. It ought to be the people who are telling lies about homosexuality and transgenderism—taking young children and giving them hormone blockers—who should be ashamed and not us. We should not be afraid to advocate the principles of God's Word.

One of the reasons I think conservatives aren't changing the nation is because Christians are so apologetic about what they believe while the liberals aren't. The ungodly are having parades to celebrate their perverted lifestyles, but Christians are afraid they will offend somebody if they stand up for the truth. Even though people are mutilating children and destroying lives, many Christians won't say anything against it.

In 2023, a professional hockey player refused to wear the homosexual pride rainbow on his uniform. His team was encouraging players to wear it to show support for the LGBTQ+XYZ. But he refused to do it because he was a Christian.

Now, I applaud him for standing his ground, but the way he did it was wrong. He said, "I respect everybody, and I respect everybody's choices. My choice is to stay true to myself and my religion."[9] By saying those things about how he respected people's choices, he just validated the homosexual lifestyle. But that's not right. It's destroying people!

Research shows that people who identify as homosexual or bisexual are two to three times more likely to engage in suicidal behavior than the general population.[10] Partner abuse among homosexuals is dramatically higher than it is in heterosexual couples.[11] And there are all kinds of other risks. It's just a destructive lifestyle!

Christians need to express love towards homosexuals, and homosexuals can be forgiven. What I'm saying is I'm not going to validate that lifestyle. I won't say, "It's okay for you, but you need to respect me." No! That is just wrong, wrong, wrong.

'Suffer for His Sake'

For unto you it is given in the behalf of Christ, not only to believe on him, but also to suffer for his sake; having the same conflict which ye saw in me, and now hear to be in me.

Philippians 1:29–30

In America, it hasn't really cost us to be Christian— although this seems to be changing. Until recently, people were respected for being Christian. But now, Christians are the only group in America that can be persecuted and treated badly without anyone else speaking up for them. I've been the subject of many stories on the front pages of newspapers, criticizing me and our ministry.

I guarantee you, if you live godly in Christ Jesus, in whatever country you're in, you are going to suffer persecution (2 Tim. 3:12). The only Christians who are not persecuted are those who are not living godly. But if you take a real stand, if you stand up against all the ungodliness and the wokeness today, it's going to cost you something.

We have a breed of Christianity in America where people just pray and ask the Lord to forgive them, so they'll go to heaven. But in between here and heaven, many people take the path of least resistance. If being a Christian would cost them something, they wouldn't dare stand up for the truth of God's Word.

I heard a story about a Christian boy who was planning to go to a secular summer camp. His mother was worried because he had never been to anything except Christian camps. She was afraid he would be persecuted and criticized for being Christian, so she prepared him and prayed the whole time he was gone. When she picked up her son, he talked about going horseback riding, canoeing, and swimming. Then, the mother asked, "Did anybody criticize you because you were a Christian?" And the boy answered, "Oh, no. Nobody even found out!"

That may be a funny story, but it illustrates an important point. If some of you reading this were arrested for being a Christian, would there be enough evidence to convict you?

I was talking to a woman who ministers in Africa, and she said there were a hundred or more pastors who have been beheaded by terrorists. One of the pastors was told to renounce the Lord or they would behead his four-year-old son. Praise God this pastor stood strong even though they carried out this beheading.

But for every person who is being killed like that, two or three more are volunteering to take their place. Sad to say, not many Americans would do that. We need to get to where we love God more than we love ourselves. And there is freedom in that. It makes life really count when you love God more than you love yourself.

Chapter 2

Esteem Others

If there be *therefore any consolation in Christ, if any comfort of love, if any fellowship of the Spirit, if any bowels and mercies, fulfil ye my joy, that ye be likeminded, having the same love,* being *of one accord, of one mind.* Let *nothing be* done *through strife or vainglory; but in lowliness of mind let each esteem other better than themselves.*

Philippians 2:1–3

The concept of unity is off most people's radar. They don't think that the body of Christ can be of one mind, but we can. This was Paul's goal, but he recognized what was standing in the way. Most people don't have any desire to esteem others above themselves.

In 1 Corinthians 3:3, Paul said that if there's envying and division among people, it's because they are carnal and walk as men. God never intended for us to have divisions. Paul is saying, with all the Lord has done for us, we ought to humble ourselves and get along with our brothers and sisters.

The Bible says God resists the proud but gives grace to the humble (1 Pet. 5:5). But what does it mean to be humble? Humility can be defined in many ways, one of which is the absence of pride. Think of it this way: Humility conducts the grace of God like copper conducts electricity. Pride stops the flow of God's grace as an insulator stops the flow of electricity.

When you are all wrapped up in yourself, you make a very small package. If you focus only on your needs and promote yourself, you are being prideful, and God will resist you. The word *resist* means to actively fight against.[12] God is against you promoting yourself.

> *Look not every man on his own things, but every man also on the things of others.*
>
> Philippians 2:4

The key to esteeming others is to quit being focused on your situation. Get your eyes off yourself, quit thinking about yourself, and quit praying about yourself all the time.

If you let God flow through you and get to where you're more concerned about other people than you are yourself, you'll wind up being blessed more accidentally than you ever were on purpose. This is how the kingdom works (Matt. 6:33). But when you are focused on just you and your family—"my four and no more"—you are resisting the power of God.

Jesus Humbled Himself

Let this mind be in you, which was also in Christ Jesus: Who, being in the form of God, thought it not robbery to be equal with God: But made himself of no reputation, and took upon him the form of a servant, and was made in the likeness of men.

Philippians 2:5–7

Paul now uses Jesus as the supreme example of humility. If God Almighty humbled Himself, how can we do any less.

This is saying that Jesus was God manifest in the flesh (1 Tim. 3:16). The whole truth of the Gospel hangs on that fact. If Jesus were only a man, then His life would have only been worth the life of one other man. But since Jesus was God, His life could atone for the sins of the whole world.

The invisible God became visible when He entered the earth through Jesus. But although Jesus had a sinless physical body, He was still 100% God in His Spirit. This is hard for us to understand but we have to acknowledge it in order to fully appreciate Jesus humbling Himself.

God is so Awesome that no man can see him and live (Ex. 33:20). That's not because the Lord is so private, but if you were to see Him as He is, you couldn't stand it. It would kill you. It's comparable to exposing a mold to sunlight—it can't survive in the light. Likewise, we can't approach the pure light of God without it killing us.

God's glory is beyond our ability to describe or understand. God had to hide Himself because our bodies cannot handle it. The only way we can connect with God is through faith. That's awesome!

Jesus was God manifested through a physical body. He emptied Himself of His divinity. Now, in the spirit, Jesus was God. Luke 2:11 says, at Jesus' birth the angel told the shepherds,

Unto you is born this day in the city of David a Saviour, which is Christ the Lord.

Jesus was God, but He was in a physical body. It says in Luke 2:52 that Jesus *"increased in wisdom and in stature, and in favour with God and man."* His earthly body wasn't supernatural. It was totally human. It was sinless, but it was still human. He had to learn to talk and walk like anyone else. The Apostle Paul wrote,

> *Being found in fashion as a man,* [Jesus] *humbled himself.*
>
> Philippians 2:8

That means there was a time Jesus had to acknowledge that He was God. His physical mind had to accept that He was God. I'm sure that His Spirit was constantly bearing witness and because He didn't have sin, He probably didn't have the doubt and reservation that we have. Nonetheless, there was a time that He had to admit, "I am God." He had to come to this revelation and accept it by faith (Luke 2:42–46).

I'll tell you, if God Almighty humbled Himself, became a man, and lived among people, why would we think we don't need to humble ourselves and put other people ahead of us?

'Every Knee Should Bow'

> *Wherefore God also hath highly exalted him, and given him a name which is above every name: That*

> *at the name of Jesus every knee should bow, of* things
> *in heaven, and* things *in earth, and* things *under the*
> *earth; And* that *every tongue should confess that Jesus*
> *Christ* is *Lord, to the glory of God the Father.*

Philippians 2:9–11

These verses are talking about angels, people who have died and gone on to heaven, people here on the earth, and things under the earth—hell and the demonic realm. Because Jesus humbled Himself, His Father exalted Him (1 Pet. 5:5b–6).

The way up in God's kingdom is down. Jesus humbled Himself. God has exalted Him and given Him a name that is above every name in heaven, in earth, and under the earth. There is no exemption for anyone or anything from coming under the Lordship of Jesus. He is Lord of all. Because of that, every person who has ever lived on this planet will someday fall before Him and confess that Jesus is Lord.

A day is coming when all the people who are shaking their fists in the face of God will be repenting in sackcloth and ashes. They will bow their knees. But it's only in this life that a person can repent and receive salvation.

There are people who claim to be atheists, but when I was in Vietnam all the atheists were crying out to God at the top of

40

their lungs when the bombs started dropping and the bullets started flying. Everybody intuitively knows that there's a God (Rom. 1:18–20). So, there's really no such thing as an atheist. If you put a gun to an atheist's head, he's going to cry out to God.

Someday, everybody is going to confess that Jesus is Lord, but it will be too late for many. It would be better to do it now and receive the benefits of being born again instead of having to spend all eternity in hell repenting and being sorry for the way that you've lived.

Humility is just as important for the believer. If you humble yourself, God will exalt you in due time (1 Pet. 5:6). Years ago, I was attending a meeting where my friend Joe Nay was ministering. Before each of his sessions, Joe would call me on stage. I wasn't ministering, but he invited me to greet the people and say something.

On the last night of those meetings, I was invited on stage again and, in front of hundreds of people, a man came running up to me, crying and kissing my boots. That man said, "I've been telling people that you're of the devil! For days, you've been coming up here and this whole time God has been convicting me of the things I've said about you." He was begging for my forgiveness, and it was quite a spectacle!

The point I'm trying to make is, if I had fought back against those kinds of accusations, there's no way I could have gotten that kind of reaction. I humbled myself, God convicted this man, and our relationship was put back together. That's awesome! Vengeance belongs to the Lord (Rom. 12:19).

God Works in You

Wherefore, my beloved, as ye have always obeyed, not as in my presence only, but now much more in my absence, work out your own salvation with fear and trembling. For it is God which worketh in you both to will and to do of his good pleasure.

Philippians 2:12–13

God has put everything in us in Christ, and it's up to us to work it out. It's like having a well with life-giving water in it, but it's not going to do you any good if the water stays there. God puts everything we need in, and we draw it out.

Years ago, there was a commercial for Prego spaghetti sauce, and their marketing slogan was, "It's in there!" If you wanted basil, "it's in there." If you wanted garlic, "it's in there." The idea was that everything typically found in a traditional homemade sauce was already in there, so you didn't have to go looking for spices and herbs anywhere else.

Well, whatever the Lord has provided to you through grace is already in your born-again spirit. For example, if you need healing, it's already in there! If you need prosperity, it's in there! God has already given you everything that pertains unto life and godliness (2 Pet. 1:3). It's already in there, but it only comes out through the knowledge of God. You've got to draw it out.

Early on in our ministry, I got it in my heart that I wanted to see the dead raised. Through my born-again spirit, I already had raising-from-the-dead power on the inside of me (Eph. 1:18–20). But to really see it manifest in my ministry, I had to renew my mind to the truth of God's Word (Rom. 12:2). So, I went through the Bible, studied every time someone was raised from the dead, and then meditated on it until I saw myself (in my imagination) raising people from the dead just like Jesus. With the Word, I drew out what God had put inside me.

Back when I was ministering in Pritchett, Colorado, I'd been praying for a man who was paralyzed from the waist down. After some time, he got to where he could move his legs, get around, and do things. One night, this man's son came and took me to his parents' house.

As I walked in, the sheriff was there with some emergency equipment trying to get an oxygen mask ready. At about the same time, I saw the man's wife crying and praying, "Oh God, please bring him back from the dead!" The first thought that came to me was, *No way!* So, I walked over and said, "In the name of Jesus, come back into that body!" And he just sat straight up! Later, a doctor checked him out and confirmed that he was completely healed.

Over the years, I've seen multiple people raised from the dead—including my own wife and son. It wasn't because of anything special about me. It's the power of God that's in me. And God is no respecter of persons (Acts 10:34)! God will do the same through you if you just draw out what's *already in you.*

'Be Blameless and Harmless'

Do all things without murmurings and disputings: That ye may be blameless and harmless, the sons of God, without rebuke, in the midst of a crooked and perverse nation, among whom ye shine as lights in the world; holding forth the word of life; that I may rejoice in the day of Christ, that I have not run in vain, neither laboured in vain.

Philippians 2:14–16

44

The children of Israel murmured and complained. Because of that, they spent forty years in the wilderness. That was never God's will. It just goes to show that if you're a griper and a complainer, it's an indication you have not submitted yourself to God.

When you just put God first, that's what really causes you to have joy. If you're a murmurer and a complainer, it shows you are the one that's controlling your life. It's because you are trying to do everything in your own power. When you get your mind stayed upon God, He'll keep you in perfect peace (Is. 26:3). If you don't have perfect peace, it's because you are all wrapped up in yourself.

The word *"crooked"* in verse fifteen is from the Greek word *skolios*.[13] It's where we get the English word *scoliosis*, which is a curvature of the spine that keeps a person from standing up straight. Brothers and sisters, we are living in a crooked and perverse nation. We need to shine as lights in this world and stand on the Word of God.

The Word is what paints the proper picture of what we are supposed to be like and what God has done for us. If you aren't immersing yourself in the Word of God on a consistent basis, then I can guarantee you're being influenced by this world.

You can't just turn your mind off—even though some people may act like they have! A person is always thinking about something. And if your mind isn't stayed on the Lord (Is. 26:3), you're not going to have peace. You're going to be full of all the sewage of the world! And you're certainly not going to stand when persecution, for the Gospel's sake, comes.

'Rejoice with Me'

Yea, and if I be offered upon the sacrifice and service of your faith, I joy, and rejoice with you all. For the same cause also do ye joy, and rejoice with me.

Philippians 2:17–18

Paul is saying that if he goes before Nero and is killed, he and the Philippians will rejoice because he did it for the Lord's sake. Not many people think that way these days. If serving the Lord costs them something, most people will grieve about their hardship. But when you live to glorify God, His glory is all that counts.

William Tyndale translated the Bible into English in the 1500s. Doing this was against the rules of the Catholic Church, so he fled England and the wrath of King Henry VIII. But

Tyndale was eventually arrested, strangled to death, and his body was burned at the stake.[14] His last words were, "Lord, open the king of England's eyes."[15] Within one hundred years, King James had the Bible translated into English. Tyndale was the main reason for the Bible's circulation in the common language. His death ended up causing a public uproar which brought positive change.

Back during the pandemic lockdowns, I was one of the few ministers to stand up to the governor of Colorado. All across the state, churches were told they had to close because they weren't "essential." And yet, marijuana shops, liquor stores, and other ungodly businesses could stay open. The Bible says that Christians should not forsake *"the assembling of ourselves together"* (Heb. 10:25), so we told the governor our *voluntary cooperation* was over—and that caused no small stir!

If all the pastors, just in the county around Charis Bible College, had stood with me, the government officials would have backed down immediately. We wouldn't have received cease-and-desist orders. I wouldn't have been threatened with arrest. But because our ministry stood nearly alone—and won—all those churches benefited. Because we were willing to fight when everything looked like it was against us, the body of Christ won. Praise the Lord!

I think with the way our world is going, some believers may have to become martyrs. Being put in jail or worse might be the catalyst that finally wakes up the body of Christ and gets them to take a stand against ungodliness. But we're going to have to be so focused on God that we're willing to suffer to help His kingdom. Our attitude must be, *So be it.*

Don't Seek Your Own

But I trust in the Lord Jesus to send Timotheus shortly unto you, that I also may be of good comfort, when I know your state. For I have no man likeminded, who will naturally care for your state. For all seek their own, not the things which are Jesus Christ's.

Philippians 2:19–21

Timothy put Jesus and others ahead of himself, just as Paul did. That's what made him a faithful partner of Paul's. So many of our problems would be solved if we put God and other people ahead of ourselves. Paul could trust that Timothy would look after the needs of the Philippians because he was of the same mind; he didn't seek his own.

Scripture says in Proverbs 13:10,

Only by pride cometh contention: but with the well advised is *wisdom.*

It didn't say pride is a leading cause or even a major cause. The only cause for strife is pride. If people weren't so in love with themselves, they wouldn't be so hurt when something doesn't go their way.

People get convicted and come to me and ask, "Would you please cast self out of me?" No! I can't cast self out of you. Every one of us has a self, and you're going to have to live with it the rest of your life. All you can do is submit it to God.

I know who I am in Christ, but I don't have any confidence in the flesh (Phil. 3:3). I have confidence in Christ in me, and I don't trust in myself. That's healthy!

We had a man who went to Australia to help launch a Charis campus. I went there to minister and announce that the school was starting, but one hour before the meeting he came to me and said, "Don't announce that we're starting the school! I can't do it! This is bigger than me!" And I told him, "Man, that's great!"

This man was shocked! So, I continued, "That's a great attitude—that you recognize this is bigger than you—as long as you don't stop there." I said, "Now you need to let Christ make up the difference. You need to go into this thing with the attitude that, 'I can't do it, but God, I believe You are going to do it through me.'" That school ended up having one of the best launches ever, has been going strong for decades, and has hundreds of students in it!

You aren't going to find the beginning of God until you get to the end of yourself. You don't have to understand everything because it's not your ability that matters. It's your response to His ability that makes things work.

Trust Has to Be Earned

But ye know the proof of him, that, as a son with the father, he hath served with me in the gospel.

Philippians 2:22

Paul wasn't just emotionally attached to Timothy. Timothy had proven his love for the Lord and Paul through his actions. Paul's feelings toward him were not based in grace, but in Timothy's actions.

You see, Timothy had proven himself. Many people desire to have others trust them as Paul trusted Timothy, but few are willing to earn that trust. Some even get upset if that trust is not extended toward them, so they try to demand it. But often faithful people are just so busy being faithful, they never demand anything. If trust isn't given, they just work harder. Trust cannot be demanded. It has to be earned.

> *Him therefore I hope to send presently, so soon as I shall see how it will go with me. But I trust in the Lord that I also myself shall come shortly.*
>
> Philippians 2:23–24

Paul was speaking about his sentencing. He was facing possible execution at the hands of the Romans. He knew they might kill him, and he didn't want Timothy to go to the Philippians until he knew the outcome of his trial.

Likewise, our Father doesn't want to send us to proclaim His message until we have the correct message. Many people are binding the devil's hindrances to their ministry when it may be the Lord who hasn't opened doors because they don't have the complete message yet.

'Ministered to My Wants'

Yet I supposed it necessary to send to you Epaphroditus, my brother, and companion in labour, and fellowsoldier,

but your messenger, and he that ministered to my wants.
For he longed after you all, and was full of heaviness,
because that ye had heard that he had been sick. For
indeed he was sick nigh unto death: but God had mercy
on him; and not on him only, but on me also, lest I
should have sorrow upon sorrow. I sent him therefore
the more carefully, that, when ye see him again, ye may
rejoice, and that I may be the less sorrowful.

Philippians 2:25–28

Here is Paul, again thinking about the Philippians more than himself. Epaphroditus was ministering to Paul, and I'm sure it would have been a blessing to Paul if he had kept him in Rome. But in typical Paul fashion, Paul sent Epaphroditus back to Phillipi so he could comfort them and deliver a good report. Paul is still considering other people, even when he's in a bad situation himself.

According to Bible scholars, the Philippians sent Epaphroditus to Paul in Rome, bearing their gift to him (Phil. 4:18). While in Rome, he assisted Paul in his work and labored so hard that he became sick. That news got back to the Philippians, and Paul knew they would be worried about one of their own. So, once Epaphroditus recovered, Paul sent him back to Philippi with his letter.[16]

52

Receive him therefore in the Lord with all gladness; and hold such in reputation: Because for the work of Christ he was nigh unto death, not regarding his life, to supply your lack of service toward me.

Philippians 2:29–30

Paul was telling the Philippians to honor Epaphroditus. Some Christians think we aren't supposed to honor anyone but the Lord. It is true that we aren't supposed to honor anyone as much as the Lord, but the Lord said that those who honor Him, He would honor (1 Sam. 2:30). We should do the same.

These days, we idolize movie stars, athletes, and many other people who are morally bankrupt, but we need *Christian* heroes. We need to honor people like Epaphroditus, who have put their own lives in jeopardy to follow God's will for their lives. People like Epaphroditus put the needs of God and others first.

Our English word *"reputation"* was translated from the Greek word entimos, which means "valued (figuratively)."[17] We are to value those who give us godly examples. The values of this world are totally upside down. Those who value ungodly people are missing the point of what Paul was saying here.

Chapter 3

'Beware of Dogs'

Finally, my brethren, rejoice in the Lord. To write the same things to you, to me indeed is *not grievous, but for you* it is *safe. Beware of dogs, beware of evil workers, beware of the concision.*

Philippians 3:1–2

When I first got turned on to the Lord, I was so introverted that I struggled to minister to people. But I still had a fire burning on the inside of me. So, I started knocking on doors. But people would just slam them in my face.

I was knocking on a hundred doors a day, but I only got to talk to five to ten people when I was done. One day, I just determined to make the next person talk to me some way or another.

I was just believing God for an opportunity to share the Gospel. So, I went to a house where a woman opened the door only a little bit because she had a chain on it. She just looked at me and asked, "What do you want?"

I responded, "Praise God! I finally found a Christian!" And she said, "Christian? What makes you think I'm a Christian?" I said, "You've got a scripture written on your fence." So, she unlatched the chain, opened the door, walked out on her porch, and asked, "Where?"

I opened my Bible to Philippians 3:2 and said, "Right here, it says, *'Beware of dogs.'*" So, I got to read all that chapter to her before she shut the door in my face. Praise God!

This scripture really isn't talking about animals. In Matthew 15:26 Jesus calls the Syrophoenician woman a dog. Deuteronomy 23:18 calls a male prostitute a dog. When Paul said, *"Beware of dogs,"* he's talking about anybody who's outside of the covenant or is an evil person. You need to beware of them. I believe he was specifically referring to the legalistic Jews who were perverting the true Gospel.

I believe that anybody can be born again. For example, Paul persecuted the church and was killing people, but on the road to Damascus he encountered the Lord and got born again (Acts 9:1–6). So, I pray that people get saved, start living for the Lord, and become transformed by the Word of God. Because if they don't get saved, they are going to be destroyed.

That may shock some people, but when Jesus comes back, the blood of those who don't accept Him will flow to the horses' bridles for a thousand and six hundred furlongs (Rev. 14:20). That's three to four feet high for two hundred miles. And Revelation 16:6 says when the ungodly are destroyed, believers will be praising God! There is a time and place for us to stand up against ungodliness!

Stand for What Is Right

For we are the circumcision, which worship God in the spirit, and rejoice in Christ Jesus, and have no confidence in the flesh.

Philippians 3:3

Paul is talking about the seal of the covenant with the Jews—the circumcision of men. In the previous verse, he used the word *concision*, which is a play on words. It means "mutilation."[18]

He's saying if a person only went through the ritual of circumcision, but their heart wasn't right, all they did was just mutilation. This is a strong statement, and it was very offensive to the Jews. But Paul wasn't wrong.

What we see happening in our nation today is due to a lack of moral restraint. All the ungodliness in modern society has come because of Christians not standing up for the truth of God's Word. They have just been too politically correct. Our nation may have been founded on godly principles, but John Adams warned, "Our constitution was made only for a moral and religious people. It is wholly inadequate to the government of any other."[19]

I heard a few years ago about a member of Congress who tried to quote from Deuteronomy 22:5 during a debate in the U.S. House of Representatives:

The woman shall not wear that which pertaineth unto a man, neither shall a man put on a woman's garment: for all that do so are *abomination unto the Lord thy God.*

The legislation being considered would have imposed pro-transgender policies on Christian organizations. This congressman was arguing that it was wrong for people to act in a way that was contrary to biology—that the transgender movement was an offense against God.

He said the bill would "go directly against what is laid out in Scripture." But a number of other representatives criticized this person for quoting the Bible, and one went as far to say, "What any religious tradition describes as God's will is no concern of this Congress."[20] That's just so contrary to what our Founding Fathers believed and what this nation was founded on!

Psalm 36:1 says,

The transgression of the wicked saith within my heart, that there is *no fear of God before his eyes.*

The church has not been the salt and the light (Matt. 5:13–14) that we should be. However, we can learn from Paul's example, stand for what's right, and speak the truth even when it's not the convenient thing to do.

The last part of that third verse is one of Paul's most radical statements. He had no confidence in the flesh. Wow! That goes contrary to the way most people think today, even most Christians.

Most people believe positive self-esteem is absolutely necessary for a healthy life, but Paul didn't think that way. He said in Galatians 6:14,

God forbid that I should glory, save in the cross of our Lord Jesus Christ, by whom the world is crucified unto me, and I unto the world.

As Paul already said in Phil. 1:21,

For to me to live is Christ, and to die is gain.

I believe in positive Christ esteem but thinking more highly of ourselves than we ought to think (Rom. 12:3) is one of the biggest problems we have. That goes contrary to everything Paul taught in the previous chapter. I have a booklet entitled, "Self-centeredness: The Source of All Grief" that will deal with that in a lot more detail.

'Counted Loss for Christ'

Though I might also have confidence in the flesh. If any other man thinketh that he hath whereof he might trust in the flesh, I more: Circumcised the eighth day, of the stock of Israel, of the tribe of Benjamin, an Hebrew of the Hebrews; as touching the law, a Pharisee; Concerning

*zeal, persecuting the church; touching the righteousness
which is in the law, blameless.*

Philippians 3:4–6

In the natural, Paul was better than just about any of us. He
said he was, *"circumcised the eighth day,"* was a *"Hebrew of the
Hebrews,"* and *"a Pharisee."*

The Pharisees were strict when it came to the Law. They
even tithed on every spice in their garden (Matt. 23:23). They
could only walk so many steps on the Sabbath.[21] Some people
even believed that you could not have a bowel movement on the
Sabbath because it was considered work.[22]

That's where Paul was coming from. It wasn't because
Paul's flesh was not as good as other people's flesh that he had
no confidence in it. In the natural, Paul was more accomplished
than anyone of his day.

*But what things were gain to me, those I counted loss for
Christ. Yea doubtless, and I count all things* but *loss for
the excellency of the knowledge of Christ Jesus my Lord:
for whom I have suffered the loss of all things, and do
count them* but *dung, that I may win Christ.*

Philippians 3:7–8

Paul was so committed to following the Law that he persecuted the church and was willing to kill people. Paul offered sacrifices every time he sinned, and he followed all the rituals, making him blameless, not sinless. And yet, he counted it all *"loss for Christ."* Paul counted all those religious things as *"dung,"* that he *"may win Christ."* That's just amazing!

Paul was probably one of the most educated men of his day and had everything in the natural going for him, but he said it was all dung compared to knowing Christ. That's quite a word picture which illustrates something important.

Some people frame their dung and put it on the wall to show others what they've done. Many of you have trophies and awards on your mantle, but they are meaningless compared to your relationship with Jesus. Paul had more achievements than any of us. And yet, he said they weren't worth anything. His whole focus was on knowing Jesus. That's awesome!

That's one of the major secrets of Paul's life that made him who he was and it's also one of the missing ingredients in most of our lives that keep us from being who we are supposed to be.

I knew a man who had come out of the gang lifestyle in New York City. He got born again, was walking with the Lord, and saw people healed and miracles happen. But at some point, he thought his wife had been unfaithful to him (even though it wasn't true). He got so mad at God that he drove down the street, threw his Bible out the window, and went and did drugs, because that's what he did before he was born again. He even tried to kill himself!

When I went to see him in the psych ward, he started crying. He said, "God's done so much for me. How could I have done something like this?" And I just told him he had gotten into the flesh because he quit focusing on Jesus. You need to recognize that without Jesus, you are nothing.

Abiding in Christ is more important than anything else in this life. If we step out of our relationship with the Lord and live out of our flesh, we are destined to fail. It's like flying in an airplane. It's not us that's flying. The plane is flying and it's only our position in the plane that allows us to fly at 35,000 feet and 450 miles per hour. If you don't believe that, step out of the plane and see how long you fly.

Likewise, it's only our reliance upon Jesus living through us that enables us to live a victorious life. Self-love, self-dependence, and self-promotion are some of the deadliest inroads of the devil into our lives.

'That I May Know Him'

And be found in him, not having mine own righteousness, which is of the law, but that which is through the faith of Christ, the righteousness which is of God by faith: That I may know him, and the power of his resurrection, and the fellowship of his sufferings, being made conformable unto his death; If by any means I might attain unto the resurrection of the dead. Not as though I had already attained, either were already perfect: but I follow after, if that I may apprehend that for which also I am apprehended of Christ Jesus.

Philippians 3:9–12

Paul wanted to be found in Christ. It was his relationship with Jesus that gave him value. In the same way, I feel really good about my born-again self. I don't have self-esteem; I have *Christ-esteem*. I am just so thankful for what Jesus has done in me. But I guarantee you, in my flesh, I don't have anything to offer.

Notice that there is self-righteousness and a faith righteousness. Self-righteousness is necessary when it comes to relating to people and the devil, but it's grossly inadequate for approaching God (Is. 64:6). It's only the righteousness of God that is given to us through putting faith in what Jesus did which grants us access into God's grace (Rom. 5:2).

I am just amazed that God would take somebody like me—a hick from Texas—and use me. I recently heard someone say about me, "There's no energy in him," and yet they were able to receive what God has shown me. That's a blessing! If I was God, I wouldn't have chosen me, but I'm just so thankful that he did.

God's not looking for a silver vessel. He's looking for a surrendered vessel. If you can look at your life and say, "Look what I did," or "I'm a self-made man," then you haven't really trusted in Christ. You are just doing things in your own strength.

I guarantee, when you stand before the Lord, all the diplomas, degrees, and awards that you have gloried in are going to be burnt up. It's only what Jesus did through you that's going to stand the fire that will *"try every man's work"* (1 Cor. 3:10–15).

When I got started in ministry, one of the things that really blessed me was ministering in nursing homes. The people running the homes would let me just come in and preach to these people, and it turned out to be a really good experience. One lady there was always dressed to the nines. She was probably ninety years old at the time, yet she still looked beautiful and kept her hair fixed. Despite these things, she would sit there and just cry all day long.

I ministered to this woman, befriended her, and found out she had been a Methodist pastor's wife. She would say, "I used to be important! People used to think I was somebody special!" But by then, nobody would come to see her. She was just spending her golden years talking about who she used to be, sitting in that nursing home, and waiting to die.

It really gave me a different perspective on things. When this woman was younger and had a prominent position in the community, everybody thought she was special. But someday, just like this pastor's wife, every one of us is going to come to the end of ourselves. It's who we are in Christ that matters. That's all that matters.

Set a Goal for Your Life

Brethren, I count not myself to have apprehended: but this *one thing* I do, *forgetting those things which are behind, and reaching forth unto those things which are before, I press toward the mark for the prize of the high calling of God in Christ Jesus.*

Philippians 3:13–14

Paul had a goal for his life. He knew what God had called him to do and he wanted to win the prize. Sad to say, most people just want to go with the flow and are content to be average. Any old dead fish can just float downstream, but in order to reach our God potential, we have to turn around and swim upstream. God has something special for you.

God's not going to call everybody to do what I do. But I can guarantee you, God will call you to do something that is beyond your ability. If you can look at your life and explain your accomplishments according to your own ability, then I believe you've missed God's calling on your life. If your life isn't supernatural, it's superficial!

There was a woman in my Bible study in Lamar, Colorado, who was just a wife and mother. She didn't have a large ministry and most people haven't heard of her, but she was stronger than horseradish in faith.

One day, this woman's baby pulled a full-sized motorcycle over on herself, crushing her chest and her head. This little baby's head was just flattened by that motorcycle. It was a bad situation. But this woman picked up her baby, put her head back in the right shape, and commanded her to come back to life. And she did! Praise the Lord!

Back when we first met this woman, she was struggling financially. Jamie and I helped her for a time, but then she got a hold of the Word and believed what it said about prosperity. Eventually, she got the idea to create a piece of exercise equipment that looked like a skateboard with a bubble on the bottom so people could balance on it while they twisted and turned. She ended up on a television show that featured people sharing their ideas with investors, and it became a huge success!

Here she was, just a housewife in the eyes of the world, and the payments she's now receiving from her invention are astronomical. That's supernatural! Not everybody may know about her, but God had something huge for her. She just kept her focus on Jesus, and because of that she saw healings, miracles, and experienced prosperity in her life.

You see, nobody is meant to just occupy space in this world. You should live your life in a way that, when you die, somebody misses you. Paul was pressing toward the mark because he had a goal. If you don't know where you're going, any road will take you there. Having a destination will limit your choices and help you make decisions.

In a similar way, people like to talk about being "multitaskers." That just means they do multiple things poorly instead of one thing really well. If you want to destroy a man's vision, give him two! Paul wasn't that way. He was focused on *"one thing,"* and that made all the difference.

Keep Walking

Let us therefore, as many as be perfect, be thus minded: and if in any thing ye be otherwise minded, God shall reveal even this unto you.

Philippians 3:15

You may be following God, but how do you know for sure that you're doing everything that God wants you to do? You just put your attention on the Lord, seek Him with your whole heart, and stand on this verse. You pray that, if you are otherwise minded, God will reveal it to you. Then you have to trust that God is going to speak to you just as He promised. He will direct you, and He will reveal things to you when the time is right.

Nevertheless, whereto we have already attained, let us walk by the same rule, let us mind the same thing.

Philippians 3:16

Many people come to God and trust Jesus for salvation. They'll sing the song, "Just as I am, without one plea, but that thy blood was shed for me, O Lamb of God, I come."[23] They put their faith in what Jesus has done for their salvation. They receive salvation by faith in what Jesus did.

But then, when it comes to healing, they start thinking about what they need to do to please God or how they may have missed it in some area. They quit trusting in Jesus only and put faith in what they have done. When they do that, they just lose all their faith that God's going to heal them because their good works are never enough.

If you would have had that attitude when it came to salvation, you'd have never gotten born again. Paul wrote in Colossians 2:6,

As ye have therefore received Christ Jesus the Lord, so *walk ye in him.*

That means that the same way you receive salvation is the same way you receive everything else. If you've already received salvation, which is the greatest gift, and just continue to walk by faith in what Jesus has done, you won't let the devil condemn you over your mistakes and failures. You could just receive from God what He's already made available. That's powerful!

Follow Good Examples

Brethren, be followers together of me, and mark them which walk so as ye have us for an ensample. (For many walk, of whom I have told you often, and now tell you even weeping, that they are *the enemies of the cross of Christ.*

Philippians 3:17–18

If people would just do what Paul is saying in this verse, it would totally transform the body of Christ. Paul is telling people to not just listen to someone's words, but to look at their life to see if it matches up with what they are preaching.

Many ministers today will get up and preach faith, but they don't live it. If a pastor preaches one thing on Sunday but lives something differently Monday through Saturday, don't follow him!

I know that's a strong statement, but if ministers had to be judged on their lives, not just their words, it would disqualify many of them. I'll tell you, we've got a lot of unqualified people serving in ministry. I'm not against them—and God loves them—but they don't need to be in positions of leadership.

They only have those positions because the body of Christ does not follow Paul's instructions. They will go to a church because of the pastor's charisma, the music, or some other superficial reason. Instead, Paul is saying you need to follow leaders who demonstrate biblical values through what they teach and how they live.

For example, there are a lot of woke preachers out there who are using the Bible to say that Jesus would approve of abortion, homosexuality, transgenderism, and things like that. They are enemies of the cross. What's more, many pastors know the truth but just aren't saying anything against ungodliness. What they don't realize is that their silence speaks volumes.

I was once talking with a minister who had a church in San Francisco, but he didn't address the issue of homosexuality from the pulpit. He said, "I want to love these people, and I don't want to condemn anybody or turn them away."

I agree that we aren't supposed to condemn people, but I asked him, "What about the young people in your church? I can guarantee they are being taught pro-homosexual ideas in the schools. If you don't counter it, where are they going to hear the truth?" Then this pastor just looked at me said, "Well, I never thought of that."

Now, I'm not against anybody and I don't hate homosexuals, but I hate Satan who is destroying people's lives. Ministers have a God-given responsibility to speak the truth, no matter whether it is popular or not.

I once had a man come and ask me to help him with a problem. As he was sharing with me, the Lord showed me that he was the problem. The Lord showed me a number of things that this man had done which brought these things upon himself. I suspected that he wouldn't like it if I told him what the Lord had told me.

As I was debating whether or not to tell him all of this, the Lord told me that I didn't have the right to reject the truth for him. I had a responsibility to tell him what the Lord was telling me and if he rejected it, that was his choice. But I didn't have the right to reject the truth for him which is what I would have done if I had held back part of what the Lord revealed to me.

We are interpreters for the Lord. An interpreter isn't speaking for himself. He is supposed to be interpreting what the other person is saying. Any minister who won't speak forth what God says in His Word is not a faithful interpreter.

Do Not Mind Earthly Things

Whose end is *destruction, whose God* is their *belly, and* whose *glory* is *in their shame, who mind earthly things.*

Philippians 3:19

Again, many Christians just don't want to offend anybody. It's getting to where you can't say anything because people are so sensitive today. They just think you're being critical and condemning them.

A few years ago, during the pandemic, colleges gave coloring books and crayons to their students because they were just so stressed out. That's terrible. These "snowflakes" just need to pull their thumbs out of their mouths and grow up.

Paul is saying these kinds of people follow their belly as their god. That means they are doing things to satisfy their own lusts and desires. They are not consistent with what Paul has said through this whole letter. They are not loving God and loving people more than themselves. They love themselves, deny the Lord, and would do anything to promote themselves or their ministry. That's ungodly.

During the pandemic lockdowns many ministers would not stand up for what's right. And it was because they loved the praise of men more than the praises of God. Paul said people like that *"mind earthly things."*

You're supposed to let your mind, your conversation, and your thoughts be in heaven. Paul wrote in Colossians 3:1–2,

> *If ye then be risen with Christ, seek those things which are above, where Christ sitteth on the right hand of God. Set your affection on things above, not on things on the earth.*

Most Christians feel completely at home watching movies and shows featuring homosexuality, adultery, lying, stealing, and murder. I was once ministering to someone who was struggling with suicidal thoughts, and I told this person a lot of it was due to the people they associated with. I talked to another person, and they were telling me about the hard life they lived, saying, "I took Jesus places He never wanted to go."

Now, the Lord promised He would never leave nor forsake you (Heb. 13:5), but would the Lord be pleased with some of the things you're watching or doing? Would he be pleased with how you're spending time?

Look Forward to the Glorious

For our conversation is in heaven; from whence also we look for the Saviour, the Lord Jesus Christ: Who shall change our vile body, that it may be fashioned like unto his glorious body, according to the working whereby he is able even to subdue all things unto himself.

Philippians 3:20–21

Our bodies are amazing. I've actually heard that scientists can't understand why we die, because the body has the ability to heal and repair itself. They are at a loss to explain that. Of course, we know that sin causes our bodies to deteriorate and die (Rom. 6:23). But the body is still an amazing thing created by God. Yet, Paul calls it a *"vile"* thing.

It's vile in comparison to what God intended it to be and compared to what it's going to be. It's often said that people only use 10 percent of their brains. I believe God never intended for that to be the way it is. I believe that we have the capacity for much, much more.

In a sense, I believe in evolution. But it's *de*-evolution! We've evolved downward. Adam was able to name every animal in the world. That's just amazing to think about.

Even if you go back and read books from 200 or 300 years ago, most people would need a dictionary to understand them. Just a few hundred years ago, people had a vocabulary that was much stronger than ours. For example, children in the first grade could memorize and quote things that most adults today could not even comprehend. We have the capacity for more, but we just aren't living up to it.

The good news is you have a better body awaiting you. That means we shouldn't be so dependent upon satisfaction in this life. The best is yet to come.

I'm here because God has given me an assignment. I may not have finished it yet, but I'm looking forward to someday having a new body that will just zip from one side of the universe to the other, to know all things even as also I am known (1 Cor. 13:12), to have no more sorrow or crying (Rev. 21:4), and be in a state where former things will never even come to mind (Is. 65:17). If you are born again, your future is so bright you're going to have to squint to look at it!

'Be of the Same Mind'

Therefore, my brethren dearly beloved and longed for,
my joy and crown, so stand fast in the Lord, my dearly
beloved.

Philippians 4:1

Twice in the first verse of the fourth chapter, Paul talks about the Philippians as being his dearly beloved. These people were dear to him. In the first chapter, he said he rejoiced every time he thought of them, which was often. Certainly, one of the things that made them so close was their partnership with him in the Gospel, as he expounds upon in this chapter.

I beseech Euodias, and beseech Syntyche, that they be of
the same mind in the Lord.

Philippians 4:2

Paul is beseeching these two women to be of *"the same mind in the Lord."* Again, people have just kind of accepted division as a fact of life. It is true that differences may arise, as can be seen here. But notice that Paul doesn't just accept it as something inevitable. He called for unity. Division is damaging to the work of the Lord, and variances should be reconciled if possible.

Years ago, when I was pastoring, I had a guy come to me talking about the division he saw in our church. I said, "Yes, there are problems, but you're the source of it! We didn't have all these problems before you came here." That caught this guy off guard, and I thought he was going to get really mad at me, but instead he just opened up to me.

This man, who was causing all kinds of problems in the church, told me he was indicted by a grand jury three times before he was thirteen years old. He grew up in reformatories and foster homes. He said, "I don't know what normal is. Strife is normal for me."

That really enlightened me because I grew up in a home where we loved each other. But there are some people whose idea of normal is totally perverted. As a result, there's so much strife and division in our society today that we just accept it. But among believers, we are supposed to be saying the same thing, of the same mind, and of the same judgment. There is power in unity, and we need to strive for that.

> *And I intreat thee also, true yokefellow, help those women which laboured with me in the gospel, with Clement also, and* with *other my fellowlabourers, whose names* are *in the book of life.*

Philippians 4:3

Clement was a direct disciple of Paul, and Bible scholars believe he became the bishop of Rome around the end of the first century.[24] The word *yokefellow* paints a picture of someone pulling together with Paul in the work of the Gospel, like yoked oxen. The strength of the oxen is increased by being yoked together. The *Good News Translation* translates this as *"faithful partner."*

Rejoice in the Lord Always

> *Rejoice in the Lord alway:* and *again I say, Rejoice.*

Philippians 4:4

I believe the reason Paul repeated himself is because when he said, *"Rejoice in the Lord alway,"* people probably thought,

Well, he can't mean always. So, he said, *"again I say, Rejoice."* He emphasized that we are supposed to rejoice in the Lord always. And if you look that verse up in the Greek, it means "always."[25]

You can measure a person's maturity by their praise and thankfulness. Many people think if something bad happens, something's wrong with a person if they're just praising God and not falling apart like a $2 suitcase. But Paul says we can praise God through anything. Remember, Paul wrote this while he was imprisoned!

I used to minister in Charlotte, North Carolina every year. I had a partner there who owned a business, and he invited me to speak to his staff. Around twenty-five people worked for him, and he told them, "The clock's running, so you listen to this guy talk as long as he wants to!" I would minister to them, and he would give them time to come back into the breakroom so I could pray with them. We saw people healed, saved, and delivered. Great things happened!

Once a woman who tried to kill herself just a few days before I got there was in the group. It was her first day back at work, and she came to me for prayer. This woman had already been through multiple marriages and her current husband had just told her that he was going to get a divorce. She was crying and said that was the reason she tried to kill herself. "I'm not a Christian, but I know that you are, and I know that prayer works," she said. "Would you please pray for me that I would not get a divorce?"

I just looked at this woman and said, "Let me make sure I heard this right. You aren't a Christian, you know you aren't a Christian, and if you were to die, you would go to hell." And she said, "Yes, I guess I would." So, I said, "And you want me to pray for your marriage and not pray for your salvation?" And she said, "Yes!"

That's when I told her, "Lady, after you've burned in hell for a thousand years, you aren't going to give a rip whether this marriage worked or not. You've got your priorities all wrong. You need to get saved." You would have thought I slapped that woman! She just quit crying, came to her senses, and said, "I guess you're right!" So, I prayed with her, she got born again, and *then* we prayed for her marriage.

Now, I'm not saying that marriage isn't important. But I am saying that if you look at things in the light of eternity, even if you're having problems in your marriage, you could still praise God and say, "Thank You, Jesus, that in heaven they don't marry, nor are given in marriage (Matt. 22:30). Thank You that this is temporary!" You can rejoice over anything!

So, just as Paul commanded here, we should rejoice in the Lord always. There are no exceptions.

Pray with Thanksgiving

Let your moderation be known unto all men. The Lord is at hand. Be careful for nothing; but in every thing by prayer and supplication with thanksgiving let your requests be made known unto God.

Philippians 4:5–6

This is saying that we need to demonstrate our faith, and not just keep it to ourselves. We need to wear it on the outside, where people can see it. One of the ways we do that is by being *"careful for nothing."* I often have people say to me, "Be careful," or "Take care." But my response is always, "For nothing!"

You can put this together with 1 Peter 5:5–7, which says,

God resisteth the proud, and giveth grace to the humble. Humble yourselves therefore under the mighty hand of God, that he may exalt you in due time: Casting all your care upon him; for he careth for you.

Many people don't see that these things are connected, but

you can tell if you're humble by whether or not you're taking care. Maybe you stay up at night trying to figure out how to solve your problems, and think, *What am I going to do?* If that's the case, you haven't humbled yourself and cast your care over on the Lord. You are still trying to solve problems out of your own strength. You haven't put things in God's hands.

Paul says that you are supposed to *"be careful for nothing."* And if you look that up in the Greek, it means "nothing."[26] There is no reason to be careful. It doesn't matter what happens!

Notice that the emphasis is on *you*. Paul wrote this in the second person. *You* should, with thanksgiving, let your request be made known to God. That means there should never be a time that you just throw up spiritually on the Lord during your prayer time and tell Him every hurt and pain that you've got. You are supposed to let your requests be made known *"with thanksgiving."* If you can't praise God as you make your petitions, then I can guarantee you aren't in faith.

Some of you may think, *You aren't being sensitive! You aren't empathizing! You aren't feeling the hurt of other people!* Now, I've had a lot of bad things happen to me, so I'm not condemning anyone. But what you need is somebody to encourage you and lift you up instead of getting down in the dumps with you and just adding more misery to your situation.

'Keep Your Hearts and Minds'

*And the peace of God, which passeth all understanding,
shall keep your hearts and minds through Christ Jesus.*

Philippians 4:7

Jesus modeled how to pray in Matthew 6:9, when he said, *"Our Father which art in heaven, Hallowed be thy name."* He starts by praising God. Then he slips in, *"Give us this day our daily bread. And forgive us our debts"* (Matt. 6:11–12a). Then he ends it with, *"For thine is the kingdom, and the power, and the glory, for ever"* (Matt. 6:13b).

This is what I call the sandwich technique. You start with praise, which makes you focus on the answer instead of the problem. Then you slip in your problem. And then you end with praise, acknowledging God heard your prayer and answered it, because you should believe you receive when you pray (Mark 11:24).

Praise ought to be part of every prayer. You ought to be thanking and praising God, even if you are in the worst situation possible. God will turn things around!

On March 4, 2001, I received a call at 4:05 a.m. that my youngest son was dead. He was in a morgue, in a cooler, with

86

a toe tag on. I had every emotion of grief and sorrow that you could imagine. I don't deny that is how I felt. But I knew Jesus bore my grief and carried my sorrow (Is. 53:4), and I didn't have to let my emotions control me.

I started praising God out loud and thanking Him for His comfort and power. That's not how I felt, but that's what I believed. When I did that, the Spirit of God rose up inside me and my faith revived. The Lord spoke things to me that assured me he would live again. I had the *"peace of God, which passeth all understanding."* I told my wife that this was going to be the greatest miracle we had ever seen!

Sure enough, when we got to the hospital, my oldest son greeted me and told me that my youngest son sat up and started talking a few minutes after he called. There was no brain damage, even though he had been dead between four and five hours. It was a miracle that would not have happened if I had been controlled by my emotions. Thank God, we chose to praise Him!

'Think on These Things'

Finally, brethren, whatsoever things are true, whatsoever things are honest, whatsoever things are just, whatsoever things are pure, whatsoever things are lovely, whatsoever things are *of good report; if* there be *any virtue, and if* there be *any praise, think on these things.*

Philippians 4:8

This verse is nearly unbelievable. Many Christians today think, *This is way too committed to God. You just can't live this way!* Well, that may be the reason we're not having the same impact Paul had. If the Lord tarries, people won't be talking about most of us 2,000 years from now as we are talking about Paul, because we just occupied ourselves with things we shouldn't have.

It's possible that not one out of a thousand Christians even has a desire to follow this verse. Many people couldn't handle the thought of missing out on movies, sports, and social media. I'm not condemning you, but I am saying that Paul, a guy who was used so mightily of God, didn't think that way. And in the previous chapter, Paul shared the secret of his success—he focused on one thing (Phil. 3:13).

Some people criticize me because I'm so single minded on the Lord. I don't do well at games like Trivial Pursuit because I have missed out on over fifty-five years of American culture. But at the same time, I've seen the Lord do miraculous things.

Sure, I may be missing out on things—like depression, fear, and anxiety. If you do what Paul says in this verse, you're going to miss a lot. I can just picture Adam and Eve, sitting on their porch when they were 900 years old, and Eve saying, "Well, Adam, we sure learned a lot about sickness, disease, and murder, didn't we?" I bet when they looked back on their lives, they wished they had missed out on all of that.

It's going to cost you something if you want to see the fullness of God's power work in your life. You cannot keep your mind on the things of this world and still have a good attitude. You can't have peace with your mind focused on everything that this world offers you. You must think on things that are true, honest, just, pure, lovely, of good report, virtuous, and praiseworthy.

Do What You've Learned

Those things, which ye have both learned, and received, and heard, and seen in me, do: and the God of peace shall be with you.

Philippians 4:9

Every one of us ought to be able to tell people, "Look at the things that you see me doing and the things that I'm believing.

89

If you believe, it'll work for you." That's what Paul said. Some of you aren't doing what you're supposed to do, and you know it. Yet you wonder why the Lord isn't using you. It's because you aren't usable.

Now, I believe in grace. God loves you regardless of how you're living. You can't make Him love you more if you live right, and you can't make Him love you less if you don't live right. But *you* will love God less if you're not living a holy life.

You will have less of the power of God flowing through you because you aren't seeking him. You'll be clogged up with the things of this world and His power can't flow through you. God won't change His mind toward you, but your mind toward God can change if you start living a godly life. There is still a purpose for living a godly life, even though we live under a dispensation of grace.

> *But I rejoiced in the Lord greatly, that now at the last your care of me hath flourished again; wherein ye were also careful, but ye lacked opportunity.*

Philippians 4:10

Paul is talking about the gifts that came to him. When Paul was in Rome, he lived two years in prison (Acts 28:30), but not with other prisoners. He lived in a hired house that gave him some freedom and allowed him to write a good portion of the New Testament. Now, how does a prisoner pay for a house?

It was the Philippians who enabled Paul to pay for his own house, while under arrest, for two years. He couldn't work or make any money for himself, so it must have come from his partners! The Philippians sent money and gifts to Paul, ministering unto him. That's what he's referring to. He was rejoicing that their care for him had flourished again.

These people weren't clogging up the flow of God in their lives. They were generous, thinking of Paul and his needs. The Philippians were faithful partners.

'Do All Things Through Christ'

Not that I speak in respect of want: for I have learned, in whatsoever state I am, therewith *to be content. I know both how to be abased, and I know how to abound: every where and in all things I am instructed both to be full and to be hungry, both to abound and to suffer need. I can do all things through Christ which strengtheneth me.*

Philippians 4:11–13

People like to quote the thirteenth verse all the time, but you can't do just anything. You can do all things God wants you to do—anything that is God's will—through Christ. And if you take it in context with these other verses, he was talking about bearing hardship.

Many people say, "I can do all things," because they are believing for a blessing from God. But they don't want to bear the rejection and criticism of others. Well, that's one of those "things." You need to get to where you can just deal with any situation through Christ.

Years ago, I received a letter from a woman in the Huntsville, Texas, prison who was in solitary confinement for a serious crime. After she first entered prison, she was depressed and discouraged because she had caused so much grief, and because she was separated from her family and had very limited human contact. But then, she had a genuine experience with the Lord and was born again. She heard our program on the radio and the message of the Gospel just totally transformed her life and attitude.

Although she had been born again, she was still in prison and in solitary confinement. She didn't have contact with other inmates or guards. Her meals were slipped to her through a slit in the door. She felt like there was no reason for her to keep living. She was constantly praying that the Lord would just take her home to heaven so she could get out of her situation.

When she heard me on the radio teaching about having a vibrant relationship with the Lord now, in this life, it changed everything. She said, "Now I understand that God loves me not just for what I can do for Him, but that God loves *me*. I can bless Him. I can minister back unto Him. I have a purpose for living!" That woman was experiencing more salvation, freedom, and liberty than most Christians who have never been in prison. Praise the Lord!

Many people in prison focus on all the things they can't do. But, like this woman, Paul was thinking about what he *could* do. He preached the Gospel to the Jewish leaders in Rome (Acts 28:17–29). Everyone in Caesar's palace heard the Gospel (Phil. 1:12–18). He had gained the favor of his captors so that they gave him his own hired house and the freedom for all his friends to come to him (Acts 28:30). Since serving Jesus was all that mattered to Paul, things were going better than ever before.

This whole letter talks about how Paul put Christ and other people first because he was dead to himself. He learned how to abase and how to abound; how to be full and hungry. Some people complain because they don't have five flat-screen televisions in their home, and here Paul was—*in prison*—saying, *"I can do all things through Christ."* That's powerful.

Also, many people take the *"through Christ"* off this verse and they just say, "I can do all things." They are self-confident. But, you see, your self-confidence is no good. You need to get to where your confidence is not in yourself—in the flesh—but totally in God.

All ability in the Christian life is found in Christ. It is not our ability that makes us strong, but our availability through Christ that enables us. Paul said, *"For when I am weak, then am I strong"* (2 Cor. 12:10). He was saying that when he recognized his inability and therefore relied on the Lord, then the Lord's strength flowed through him.

We can do all things *"through Christ."*

Contentment Over Circumstances

Notwithstanding ye have well done, that ye did communicate with my affliction.

Philippians 4:14

Paul had just said that whatever his circumstances were, he was content. He hastened to add that the Philippians had done the right thing in giving toward his needs. The Apostle John said,

> *But whoso hath this world's good, and seeth his brother have need, and shutteth up his bowels* of compassion *from him, how dwelleth the love of God in him?*
>
> 1 John 3:17

It is godly to give to those in need and especially to ministers who have been a blessing to you.

Notice that Paul called his lack of having physical necessities an *"affliction."* He certainly would have given to someone else in his situation. It wasn't necessary for Paul to have everything going according to God's perfect plan for him to be content.

When I served in the army in Vietnam, I lived in a bunker for thirteen months. Every night, cockroaches crawled all over me. I would use a boot as a club to kill them, just so I could get some sleep. I lived that way for more than a year. I'm glad I don't have to do that now, but I could do it. I can live anywhere, and I've learned to be content (Phil. 4:11).

95

Contentment is a choice. Paul was in prison in Rome and facing execution, but he was content. One of the ways we learn contentment is to be thankful for what we have and quit thinking about what we don't have.

Give Where You Are Fed

Now ye Philippians know also, that in the beginning of the gospel, when I departed from Macedonia, no church communicated with me as concerning giving and receiving, but ye only. For even in Thessalonica ye sent once and again unto my necessity.

Philippians 4:15–16

When Paul left Philippi, he went directly to Thessalonica, and the Philippians still supported him—but they were the only church who did that after he left the local area. I think that's tragic.

If somebody ministers something good to you from the Word of God, you're supposed to give back to them (Gal. 6:6). One of the reasons the body of Christ is in such a mess is because people give where they're begged, where they're condemned, or where they feel obligated, instead of where they are fed spiritually. In the same way, you shouldn't eat at McDonalds, then go across the street and pay at Wendy's. You should give where you're fed.

I was at a woman's house one time, and she showed me a letter. It was sent from a minister who supposedly addressed the letter to her and said, "God woke me up at three o'clock this morning and told me that you were believing for someone to be saved, someone that you love. And if you will send a $1,000 offering today, God has told me your loved one will be saved!" This lady's name was interspersed throughout the entire letter, as if that minister was writing directly to her.

Here was this woman, crying, and saying to me, "I've been praying and believing for someone to be saved, and I know that this must be God because He woke up this man at three in the morning and told him this. But I don't have $1,000! What do I do?" I could tell she was heartbroken, so I just took that letter, tore it into pieces, and threw it in the trash. I said, "That's what you do!"

I told her, "This man didn't wake up at three o'clock in the morning and get your name from God. This is a computer-generated letter!" I've been around a lot of ministers, and I've seen a lot of things. I realized that if she gave to this minister, she would give for the wrong reasons.

People only use these tactics because they work. But Christians could solve these problems just by giving where they're fed. Ministers who are condemning people or manipulating them are not feeding the body of Christ. If you would just give where you're fed, crooks like that minister would be put out of business or they would have to get right with God. It would change things.

Giving Is Sweet

Not because I desire a gift: but I desire fruit that may abound to your account. But I have all, and abound: I am full, having received of Epaphroditus the things which were sent *from you, an odour of a sweet smell, a sacrifice acceptable, wellpleasing to God.*

Philippians 4:17–18

Paul wasn't just rejoicing because his partners had supplied his needs. He was rejoicing for them because he knew their giving would produce fruit that would abound to their account. It's obvious how our giving blesses the person we give to, but it takes faith to see how our giving also blesses us.

If you can't do that which is least, you can't do that which is greatest (Luke 16:10). If you aren't trusting God in your finances, it's hindering you in healing, joy, peace, relationships, and everything else. Trusting God with your finances is the absolute least use of your faith. That's not for the super saint; it's for baby Christians. In the Christian life, it's the bottom rung on the ladder, not the top rung. Those are amazing statements!

Years ago, I was ministering in Yucaipa, California, on these things. Even though they had already received an offering that night, I said, "I'm going to receive another offering, just to give you an opportunity to act on the things I taught. But, so you won't think I preached on this for selfish reasons, it'll all go to the church. I'm not going to take a penny of it."

While I was sitting down and they were passing the buckets, the Lord spoke to me. He said, "Watch, because people have started taking steps of faith. Look at what happens." And miracles started happening around that church just like popcorn. People started jumping up because they were healed. We saw two totally deaf people instantly healed. As a result, we had four people run to the front to accept Jesus as Lord and Savior, because they saw the power of God at work. I didn't even have to give an invitation! It was awesome!

Paul also said that when the Philippians gave, it produced a sweet odor like a sacrifice. In the spiritual realm, being generous produces a smell that pleases God. Conversely, being greedy puts out a smell just like excrement. Now, I've heard that flies can smell those kinds of things from miles away. They're just attracted to it. When you are a stingy person, holding on to everything, and just thinking about yourself, you put out an odor that draws every demon from around the county. It attracts problems!

Sometimes, I'll minister to people who always seem to have a problem. I don't mind helping them, but their *main* problem is that their attitude stinks, and it just draws demonic things into their life. It doesn't matter how much money you give to someone like that, because they'll continue attracting problems. And it always goes back to their giving.

When you give, it's a sweet smell; it's a sweet odor to God. It draws the blessing of God. When you're stingy, it draws the demonic into your life.

'My God Shall Supply'

But my God shall supply all your need according to his riches in glory by Christ Jesus.

Philippians 4:19

Many people try and take this verse and apply it to themselves; that God's going to supply all their needs. But it doesn't apply to everybody. That's a promise to partners, to people who were giving to Paul on a regular basis.

If you aren't trusting God with your finances, and you operate in fear instead of faith, you aren't going to see the flow of God's supply. It's not because God doesn't love you, and it's not because He hasn't made the supply available. It's just that you aren't cooperating.

If I put a million dollars in your bank account, it wouldn't do you any good if you didn't make a withdrawal. There are things that you have to do, and if you don't draw it out, you could end up in the poor house. You could have your house and car repossessed with a million dollars in the bank, if you don't know how to draw that money out.

In the same way, God has placed everything you need in your born-again spirit. You have prosperity, healing, deliverance, and raising-from-the-dead power inside you, but you've got to cooperate. You have to start living to give. If you haven't gotten to a place where you would rather give than receive (Acts 20:35), then you are hindering God's blessings and the promise of this verse doesn't apply.

God has blessed us with all spiritual blessings (Eph 1:3), but people who become partners go beyond themselves and recognize that money isn't just for them. It's not just there to get all their needs met. Money empowers Christians to be a blessing, so they can help others.

This promise only applied to partners—people who were not just giving to Paul once or twice, but those who were supporting him while he was in prison for two years and paying for all his expenses. Those are the people whose needs would be supplied by God.

You'll learn that if God can get it through you, He will get it to you. But if you build a dam and start holding it up, you'll stop the flow of God's blessing.

Unto God Be the Glory

Now unto God and our Father be glory for ever and ever. Amen. Salute every saint in Christ Jesus. The brethren which are with me greet you. All the saints salute you, chiefly they that are of Caesar's household. The grace of our Lord Jesus Christ be with you all. Amen.

Philippians 4:20–23

That's amazing! Paul got people born again in Caesar's household; people who would have gone to hell. Instead of griping and murmuring about his imprisonment, Paul used it as an opportunity to glorify God. Because of that, people in the household of Caesar—the emperor of the most powerful nation on the planet at that time—got born again.

This letter gives us insight into how Paul lived and how he was able to accomplish what he did. These things worked for Paul, and God is no respecter of persons (Rom. 2:11). If he did it for the Apostle Paul, he'll do it for you if you have the same attitude and commitment.

More than 150 years ago, Dwight L. Moody was in a service and heard the preacher Henry Varley say, "The world has yet to see what God can do through a man who is totally yielded to Him." Moody only had a fifth-grade education, worked selling shoes, and was volunteering as a janitor at the YMCA. But he said, "By the Grace of God, I will be that man!"[27]

Like Paul, Dwight L. Moody just went out and changed the whole world. He established ministries on nearly every continent and spoke to nearly every leader in the world, all without television, radio, or the internet. Millions of people were born again through one person who let God use him. That's awesome!

A Christian's attitude ought to be, *God, look no further. Here I am. Send me* (Is. 6:8). If you would make the same decisions that Paul made—that to live is Christ and to die is gain (Phil. 1:21) and to esteem other people better than yourself (Phil. 2:3)—then you could do all things through Christ (Phil 4:13). And I guarantee you, miracles will happen. Praise the Lord!

Conclusion

The Apostle Paul put the kingdom of God ahead of his own kingdom. He was finding joy and peace, even in being a prisoner, because people were being born again. Just like Paul, it ought to be our heart to bless God, be a servant to God, and to let God flow through us.

If people are being touched by our witness, even if it's to our detriment, we should find joy in that. If somebody got blessed through us standing up for the truth and not bowing the knee, God will show up and people will be born again because of it. That's what Paul was rejoicing in throughout this letter to his partners. That is why Philippians is such a powerful book.

Paul wrote half of the books in the New Testament, and here we are two thousand years later still talking about him. I guarantee that wasn't coincidental. It was because of the work of God in his life.

You see, Paul didn't have any confidence in his flesh (Phil 3:3). He took all his great accomplishments and the love that he had for himself, and he counted it all as dung (Phil 3:8). Paul just sought to know Christ and be found in Him. That's an attitude that every one of us needs!

I really encourage you to take the lessons found in Philippians and apply them to your own life. God is no respecter of persons, and what He did for Paul, I believe He'll do for you!

FURTHER STUDY

If you enjoyed this booklet and would like to learn more about some of the things I've shared, I suggest my teachings:

1. *Grace: The Power of the Gospel*
2. *The Power of Partnership*
3. *Financial Breakthroughs*
4. *Christian Philosophy*
5. *Observing All Things*
6. *Self-Centeredness: The Source of All Grief*

These teachings are available free of charge at **awmi.net** or for purchase at **awmi.net/store**.

Receive Jesus as Your Savior

Choosing to receive Jesus Christ as your Lord and Savior is the most important decision you'll ever make!

God's Word promises, *"That if thou shalt confess with thy mouth the Lord Jesus, and shalt believe in thine heart that God hath raised him from the dead, thou shalt be saved. For with the heart man believeth unto righteousness; and with the mouth confession is made unto salvation"* (Rom. 10:9–10). *"For whosoever shall call upon the name of the Lord shall be saved"* (Rom. 10:13). By His grace, God has already done everything to provide salvation. Your part is simply to believe and receive.

Pray out loud: "Jesus, I acknowledge that I've sinned and need to receive what you did for the forgiveness of my sins. I confess that You are my Lord and Savior. I believe in my heart that God raised You from the dead. By faith in Your Word, I receive salvation now. Thank You for saving me."

The very moment you commit your life to Jesus Christ, the truth of His Word instantly comes to pass in your spirit. Now that you're born again, there's a brand-new you!

Please contact us and let us know that you've prayed to receive Jesus as your Savior. We'd like to send you some free materials to help you on your new journey. Call our Helpline: **719-635-1111** (available 24 hours a day, seven days a week) to speak to a staff member who is here to help you understand and grow in your new relationship with the Lord.

Welcome to your new life!

Receive the Holy Spirit

As His child, your loving heavenly Father wants to give you the supernatural power you need to live a new life. *"For every one that asketh receiveth; and he that seeketh findeth; and to him that knocketh it shall be opened...how much more shall* your *heavenly Father give the Holy Spirit to them that ask him?"* (Luke 11:10–13).

All you have to do is ask, believe, and receive!

Pray this: "Father, I recognize my need for Your power to live a new life. Please fill me with Your Holy Spirit. By faith, I receive it right now. Thank You for baptizing me. Holy Spirit, You are welcome in my life."

Some syllables from a language you don't recognize will rise up from your heart to your mouth (1 Cor. 14:14). As you speak them out loud by faith, you're releasing God's power from within and building yourself up in the spirit (1 Cor. 14:4). You can do this whenever and wherever you like.

It doesn't really matter whether you felt anything or not when you prayed to receive the Lord and His Spirit. If you believed in your heart that you received, then God's Word promises you did. *"Therefore I say unto you, What things soever ye desire, when ye pray, believe that ye receive* them, *and ye shall have* them" (Mark 11:24). God always honors His Word—believe it!

We would like to rejoice with you, pray with you, and answer any questions to help you understand more fully what has taken place in your life!

Please contact us to let us know that you've prayed to be filled with the Holy Spirit and to request the book *The New You & the Holy Spirit.* This book will explain in more detail about the benefits of being filled with the Holy Spirit and speaking in tongues. Call our Helpline: **719-635-1111** (available 24 hours a day, seven days a week).

Call for Prayer

If you need prayer for any reason, you can call our Helpline, 24 hours a day, seven days a week at **719-635-1111**. A trained prayer minister will answer your call and pray with you.

Every day, we receive testimonies of healings and other miracles from our Helpline, and we are ministering God's nearly-too-good-to-be-true message of the Gospel to more people than ever. So, I encourage you to call today!

About the Author

Andrew Wommack's life was forever changed the moment he encountered the supernatural love of God on March 23, 1968. As a renowned Bible teacher and author, Andrew has made it his mission to change the way the world sees God.

Andrew's vision is to go as far and deep with the Gospel as possible. His message goes far through the *Gospel Truth* television program, which is available to over half the world's population. The message goes deep through discipleship at Charis Bible College, headquartered in Woodland Park, Colorado. Founded in 1994, Charis has campuses across the United States and around the globe.

Andrew also has an extensive library of teaching materials in print, audio, and video. More than 200,000 hours of free teachings can be accessed at **awmi.net**.

Endnotes

1. *Strong's Exhaustive Concordance of the Bible*, "G2842, koinónia: fellowship," accessed November 29, 2023, https://biblehub.com/greek/2842.htm.

2. *Strong's Definitions*, s.v. "εἰλικρινής" ("eilikrinēs"), accessed January 23, 2024, https://www.blueletterbible.org/lexicon/g1506/kjv/tr/0-1/.

3. Johnson Oatman, "Count Your Blessings," 1897.

4. *Blue Letter Bible*, s.v. "joy," accessed December 13, 2023, https://www.blueletterbible.org/search/search.cfm?Criteria=joy&t=KJV#s_primary_50_1.

5. *Blue Letter Bible*, s.v. "rejoice," accessed December 13, 2023, https://www.blueletterbible.org/search/search.cfm?Criteria=rejoice&t=KJV#s_primary_50_1.

6. *Blue Letter Bible*, s.v. "rejoicing," accessed December 13, 2023, https://www.blueletterbible.org/search/search.cfm?-Criteria=rejoicing&t=KJV#s_primary_50_1.

7. *Blue Letter Bible*, s.v. "rejoiced," accessed December 14, 2023, https://www.blueletterbible.org/search/search.cfm?Criteria=rejoiced&t=KJV#s=s_primary_50_1.

8. Savannah Barry, "Duty is ours, results are God's," Patriot Academy, accessed February 15, 2024, https://www.patriotacademy.com/duty-is-ours-results-are-gods/

9. Dillon Burroughs, "'True To Myself And My Religion': NHL Player Ivan Provorov Refuses To Participate In Team's 'Pride Night' Festivities," *Daily Wire*, January 18, 2023, https://www.dailywire.com/news/true-to-myself-and-my-religion-nhl-player-ivan-provorov-refuses-to-participate-in-teams-pride-night-festivities.

10. Antony Chum, Chungah Kim, Andrew Nielsen, et al., "Disparities in Suicide-Related Behaviors Across Sexual Orientations by Gender: A Retrospective Cohort Study Using Linked Health Administrative Data," *American Journal of Psychiatry*, 180, No. 9 (September 2023): 660-667, https://doi.org/10.1176/appi.ajp.20220763.

11. Paul Cameron, "Domestic Violence among Homosexual Partners," *Psychological Reports*, 93, No. 2 (October 2003): 410-416, https://doi.org/10.2466/pr0.2003.93.2.410 and Betty Jo Barrett, "Domestic Violence in the LGBT Community," *Encyclopedia of Social Work*, March 2, 2015, https://doi.org/10.1093/acrefore/9780199975839.013.1133.

12. *Collins Dictionary*, s.v. "resist," accessed December 14, 2023, https://www.collinsdictionary.com/us/dictionary/english/resist.

13. *Blue Letter Bible*, s.v. "σκολιός" ("skolios"), accessed January 22, 2024, https://www.blueletterbible.org/lexicon/g4646/kjv/tr/0-1/.

14. *Encyclopedia Britannica*, s.v. "William Tyndale," accessed January 22, 2024, https://www.britannica.com/biography/William-Tyndale.

15. Steven Lawson, "William Tyndale's Final Words," Ligonier Ministries, February 18, 2015, https://www.ligonier.org/learn/articles/william-tyndales-final-words.

16. *International Standard Bible Encyclopedia*, s.v. "Epaphroditus," accessed January 22, 2024, https://www.blueletterbible.org/search/Dictionary/viewTopic.cfm?topic=IT0003129.

17. *Strong's Definitions*, s.v. "ἔντιμος" ("entimos"), accessed January 22, 2024, https://www.blueletterbible.org/lexicon/g1784/kjv/tr/0-1/.

18. *Thayer's Greek Lexicon*, s.v. "κατατομή" ("katatomē"), accessed December 11, 2023, https://www.blueletterbible.org/lexicon/g2699/kjv/tr/0-1/.

19. "Letter from John Adams to Massachusetts Militia, 11 October 1798," *Founders Online*, National Historical Publications and Records Commission, the National Archives, accessed January 4, 2024, https://founders.archives.gov/documents/Adams/99-02-02-3102.

20. Tony Perkins, "Nadler on God: He's 'No Concern of This Congress,'" Family Research Council, March 1, 2021, https://www.frc.org/updatearticle/20210301/nadler-god.

21. *Merriam-Webster Dictionary*, s.v. "Sabbath-day's journey," accessed December 11, 2023, https://www.merriam-webster.com/dictionary/sabbath-day%27s%20journey.

22. Robert M. Johnston, "The Sabbath in Late Judaism and Early Christianity," *Shabbat Shalom*, (August 1996): 24–26, https://digitalcommons.andrews.edu/cgi/viewcontent.cgi?article=1078&context=shabbat-shalom.

23. Charlotte Elliott, "Just as I Am," 1835.

24. *Smith's Bible Dictionary*, s.v. "Clement," accessed February 15, 2024, https://www.blueletterbible.org/search/Dictionary/viewTopic.cfm?topic=BT0001012

25. *Thayer's Greek Lexicon*, s.v. "πάντοτε" ("pantote"), accessed December 12, 2023, https://www.blueletterbible.org/lexicon/g3842/kjv/tr/0-1/.

26. *Strong's Definitions*, s.v. "μηδείς" ("mēdeis"), accessed January 23, 2024, https://www.blueletterbible.org/lexicon/g3367/kjv/tr/0-1/.

27. Erwin W. Lutzer, "Totally Yielded to God," Moody Church Media, 2014, https://www.moodymedia.org/articles/moody-man-our-times/, and "D.L. Moody," Moody Bible Institute, accessed December 14, 2023, https://www.moody.edu/about/our-bold-legacy/d-l-moody/.

Contact Information

Andrew Wommack Ministries, Inc.

PO Box 3333
Colorado Springs, CO 80934-3333
info@awmi.net
awmi.net

Helpline: 719-635-1111 (available 24/7)

Charis Bible College

info@charisbiblecollege.org
844-360-9577
CharisBibleCollege.org

For a complete list of all of our offices,
visit **awmi.net/contact-us**.

Connect with us on social media.

There's more on the website!

Discover FREE teachings, testimonies, and more by scanning the QR code.

Continue to grow in the Word of God! You'll be blessed!

ANDREW WOMMACK MINISTRIES

Your monthly giving makes the greatest kingdom impact.

When you give, you make an impact in the kingdom that lasts for generations. Your generosity enables our phone ministers to answer calls 24/7. Your support is also expanding Charis Bible College and allowing *The Gospel Truth* to reach an even wider global audience. You do this and more through your giving each month!

Become a Grace Partner today!
Scan the QR code or call our Helpline at 719-635-1111 and select option five for Partnershi

Andrew's
LIVING
COMMENTARY
BIBLE SOFTWARE

Andrew Wommack's *Living Commentary* Bible study software is a user-friendly, downloadable program. It's like reading the Bible with Andrew at your side, sharing his revelation with you verse by verse.

Main features:
- Bible study software with a grace-and-faith perspective
- Over 26,000 notes by Andrew on verses from Genesis through Revelation
- *Matthew Henry's Concise Commentary*
- 12 Bible versions
- 2 concordances: *Englishman's Concordance* and *Strong's Concordance*
- 2 dictionaries: *Collaborative International Dictionary* and *Holman's Dictionary*
- Atlas with biblical maps
- Bible and *Living Commentary* statistics
- Quick navigation, including history of verses
- Robust search capabilities (for the Bible and Andrew's notes)
- "Living" (i.e., constantly updated and expanding)
- Ability to create personal notes

Whether you're new to studying the Bible or a seasoned Bible scholar, you'll gain a deeper revelation of the Word from a grace-and-faith perspective.

Purchase Andrew's *Living Commentary* today at **awmi.net/living**, and grow in the Word with Andrew.

Item code: 8350

God Wants You Well book

In this book, Andrew reveals the truth of what God's unconditional love and grace has already provided. Healing is a big part of that provision. So why does religion tell you that God uses sickness to teach you something? It even tries to make you believe that sickness is a blessing. That's just not true! God wants you well! If you or someone you know needs healing, this book is for you.

The Believer's Authority book

Dig into the scriptures with Andrew as he uncovers the spiritual significance of your choices, words, and actions. He explores how they affect your ability to stand against the attacks of Satan and to receive God's best. Discover the powerful truths behind true spiritual authority and begin seeing real results.

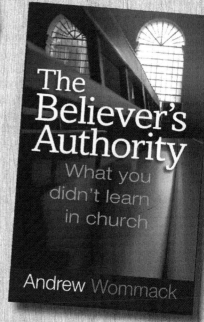